Numbers 1 - 21:
A Collection of
Questionable
Tankas and Haikus

Kim Tomlinson

Numbers 1 - 21 : A Collection of
Questionable Tankas and Haikus © 2022
Kim Tomlinson

Presentation by *BookLeaf Publishing*

Web: www.bookleafpub.com

E-mail: info@bookleafpub.com

ISBN: 978-93-95890-19-9

First edition 2022

To my parents, who have always believed in me, even when I haven't (so, a lot!)

ACKNOWLEDGEMENT

Writing East Midlands, for reigniting a passion for writing that had waned - particularly Aoife Mannix - and for enabling connection with other neurodiverse writers.

All of my secondary English teachers, to whom I expressed my dislike of poetry, but they still thought I was semi-competent at the subject.

1.

Ah, the beginning!
Wanting something meaningful?
Sorry, I've got nowt...

2.

2

Not a big issue,
Turning forty just happened.
Just the next number.
One more trip around the sun,
In the midst of a lockdown.

3.

3

Interlocking bricks.
Structured creativity.
Easy or tricky?
Follow the instructions, or
Go rogue and do your own thing!

4.

Too noisy, too hot,
Too high a chance of contact.
Best stay home instead.
Senses rest and recover.
Until next time you go out.

5.

5

This bundle of fur,
All fresh and new and hopeful.
Our little guy, Gabe.
He didn't sleep in the car -
Too much to look forward to!

6.

6

Not so little guy,
Part puppy, part bite-y fiend,
Learning all the time.
Frustrates in new ways each day,
But also brings so much love.

7.

Research the project.
Collect the materials.
Measure twice, cut once.
Never actually start -
Your time to do it is gone!

8.

8

Lying there again,
Awake, despite fighting it.
Are 3 hours enough??

9.

9

Shaping children's minds!
More like...managing parents,
Planning and marking,
Even more hoops to jump through...
When does the teaching happen?

10.

10

Always on the go,
Always moving and busy,
Always things to do.
City living isn't dull,
But not relaxing either.

11.

11

Much more relaxing,
But there's still a lot of noise
In the quietness.
Busy in different ways...
The views are nicer at least!

12.

12

Trying to decode
The meaning of peoples' words...
Is exhausting work!

13.

13

Pushed to a breakdown,
No longer able to teach,
No bandwidth for it.
Huge guilt, as usual, but
More important not to drown.

14.

14

For information,
To escape for a moment,
Just for enjoyment.
The ability to read
Will never leave you lonely.

15.

How do you manage
A brain that is always 'on'?
Double speed at that!
Catch the important Post-Its,
Let the rest land wherever.

16.

16

There are times in life
When talking to a small child
Is the best tonic -
Nobody can be too sad
Talking about unicorns.

17.

17

Severe head pain,
Added nausea and weakness,
Sometimes a light show...
How long is recovery?
Could be one day...could be four...

18.

18

A secret for you:
Busy brains and new hobbies
Mean hours of research
(Methods, supplies, and so on)
But little time doing things.

19.

When anxiety
Is kept in check by routine,
Then change is scary!
Not always the change itself,
But the impact it might have.

20.

Our lynchpin has died.
The nation is in mourning.
A new monarch reigns.

21.

Moving on in life -
Making decisions - is hard:
Which path should you take?
Next steps are never easy,
They're always to the unknown.